ABOUT THIS GUIDE

This guide is an extract from the rock climbing community database at www.thecrag.com for: World > North America > United States > Utah > Wasatch Front > North Wasatch Region > Schoolroom Area. **This guide is for personal use only. You may not sell or redistribute this guide without explicit permission from the publisher.**

Contributors

Content for this guide has been provided through www.thecrag.com.

COPYRIGHT

Difficulty ratings: By default United States of America uses the Yosemite Decimal System (YDS).

Inside Page: Author Gerald Johnson throwing down the crux on Ogden's ultra-classic Teardrops On The City (11a/b pg40).

Photo Credit: Fernando Cauldron

Cover: Alcove looking south.

Table of contents

Dedication:

This book is dedicated in memoriam of Scott Miller whose joy & enthusiasm for Ogden and all things outdoor was a continuous source of inspiration.

Introduction

Ogden's Schoolroom contains the highest concentration of established climbing along the Northern Wasatch Front. It features two tiers of quartzite cliffs nestled along Ogden's East Bench. Access is committing but the climbing is varied and rewarding for those who venture. Climbing began long before local legends Jeff and Greg Lowe started establishing classic test piece trad lines such as Tree Crack (5.11a, early 60's) and Pass or Flail (5.11d, mid 60's). Little was documented prior to mid-80's. Sport development began proliferating ~2000's. Most climbs begin on the upper tier (4x4 ledge), with a few approach pitches through the lower band. Onsight climbing can be difficult and seem sandbagged. This area has west aspect, open exposure, with longer approaches and egress requiring a fair amount of navigating. Plan accordingly and strategically. The reward is an unapparelled, intimate setting with astounding views. Climbing along Ogden's Schoolroom is rewarding, well worth the effort, and offers something for everyone.

Warning: Variable rock quality & goats are present. Be vigilant with helmets & protection. Also consider stick-clips & belay anchors as ledges can be narrow & exposed. Late spring to early fall sees insects in various trads features.

Approaches: 45-60 min, Late morning sun, Steep hike, Not kid friendly, Quartzite

Northern approach: Parking 22nd Street Trailhead:

Follow Bonneville Shoreline Trail to location (41.2259478, -111.9270853). Trail marker will indicate approach trail to the Ramp.

North Alcove: Parking 24th St or Lake St as for boulder field:

Follow trail system to Patriot crack/ Current Affairs boulders aiming for talus field near the toe on North side of Alcove (41.2224093, -111.9264163). Navigate talus field toward short trad approach pitch. Choose an appealing line to gain the Basement and 4x4 ledge system.

Southern Approach: Parking 27th Street Trailhead:

Hike Bonneville Shoreline Trail to (41.216091, -111.925324) and continue through Upper Boulderfield aiming for the Crack boulder at the base of talus field. Continue up talus field aiming toward (41.2182174, -111.9234957). Once you reach Utahnics several options exist.

Opt. 1: Climb one of the Utahnics routes to gain 4X4 ledge.

Opt. 2: Start on Hyper Dependent and continue up and left on exposed class IV/ 5 easy terrain where two bolts are available.

Opt. 3: Use Approach Routes to gain 4X4 ledge.

SCHOOLROOM OVERVIEW

SEASONALITY

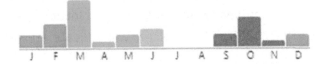

GRADE PROFILE

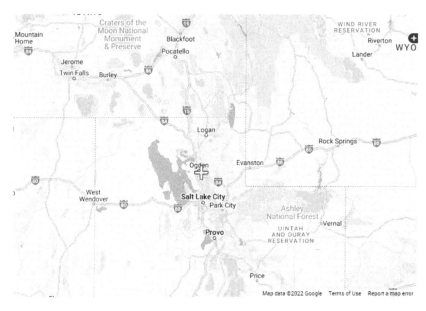

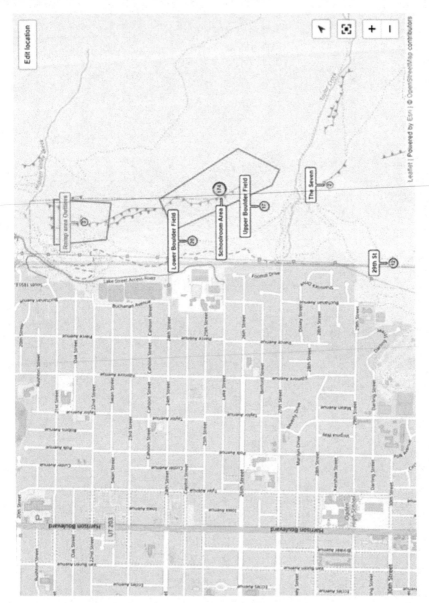

View of Schoolroom cliffband

Summary: 30-60 min, Afternoon sun, Vertical/Overhung

Description: Located north of ramp routes Graffiti Cave is easily spotted from 22nd Street Trailhead. Excellent, sustained climbing. These routes are also documented mixed lines.

Top-out has single access bolt, tree, and natural protection for accessing anchors.

Approach: Navigate to (41.2269529, -111.9275271) then proceed on foot trail leading toward cliff. Pass two impediments by scrambling through or skirting around.

1	Class IV	Schoolroom Ridge Trad

Elevation gain <750ft

Ridge scramble north of Graffiti Cave. Approach as for Graffiti Cave then cut north toward the cliff toe. Follow the most appealing route. Class V segments exist for the initiated or bypassed if desired.

Egress

-North: Hike northeast/ east to gain hidden valley trail

-Southwest: Navigate down gully, aiming for Graffiti Cave. Either repel or scramble to base of Graffiti Cave.

Graffiti Cave

5.7   Graffiti Slab 30m Trad

South facing, broken slab left of Graffiti Cave with various lines to choose. Mostly ~5.6 climbing with harder moves through midsection. Start low below the graffiti cave ledge and avoid the corner. Angle right toward belay tree. Walk off to Graffiti Cave repel or scramble to base.

Standard rack

1. Graffiti Cave

3   **5.10d/11a**   Love Peace Weed 15m Sport 5blt
                         Start in corner then move right onto steep face.

4   **5.12a**   MIA 18m Sport 8blt
                         Climbs out from cave.

5   **5.11b/c**   Take Care of Her 18m Sport 6blt
                         Climbs face.

6   **5.9**   Lunch Box RIP 15m Sport 6blt
                         Follow ramp up and left, finish on steep face.

2. The Ramp

Summary: 30-45 min, Late-morning sun

Description: Two separated crags encountered ~2/3rd distance along Schoolroom's northern ramp.

Approach: Same a Schoolroom North (pg9). Navigate Bonneville Shoreline Trail to foot trail near (41.223944, -111.924889). Continue on steepening foot trail up ramp.

1	5.9	Homecoming Princess 18m Sport 5blt
		Climb broken face trending right at 5th bolt.
2	5.9	Blue Steel 18m Sport 4blt
		Climbs up through 2 bulges.
3	5.10a	Interstellar 18m Sport 5blt
		Pushes through small roof with sustained climbing above.
4	5.9	Phantasmagorical Direct 18m Sport 4blt
		Pulls left of roof near 2nd bolt.
5	5.7	Phantasmagorical var. 18m Sport 4blt
		Climb right face (5.7) near 2nd bolt, pulling around and continuing up arete.
6	5.9 PG13	Catharsis 18m Trad
		Climb through roof then follow left leading crack on upper face.
		Rack to #1
7	5.10a PG13	Alienation Effect 18m Trad
		Same start as Catharsis. Trend right moving through features on upper face.
		Rack to #1

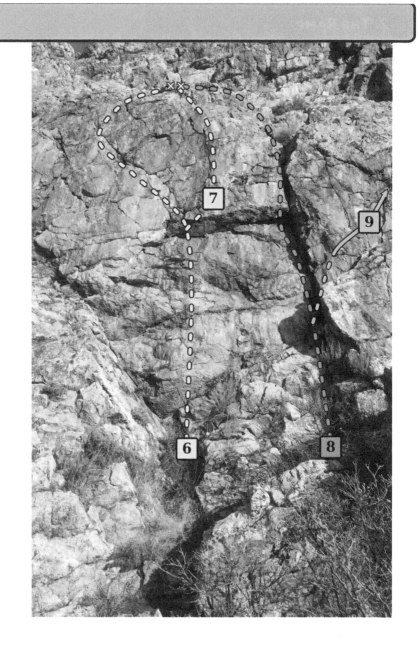

8   5.10a   FDR 15m Trad
Obvious widening crack on right side
Rack to #2

9   5.5   Dork Crack 20m Trad
An arbitrary route. Follows flakes right trending in semi-circle back to ground level.
Standard rack

The Ramp in Winter. Excellent conditions can be found on the sun baked walls even during cold weather.

3. SUNDAY WALL

Summary: 30-60 min, Late-morning/ Afternoon sun, Low angle/Moderate

Description: Located atop the ramp's prow you will find excellent introduction to trad moderate routes.

Approach: Same a Schoolroom North approach (pg9). Navigate Bonneville Shoreline Trail to foot trail near (41.223944, -111.924889). Continue on steepening trail until ramp apex.

1	5.5	**Super Bowl Sunday 23m Trad** Climb flakes heading left up slab. Build belay on ledge. Descend via Sunday School belay a short distance to the south. Rack to #3
2	5.7	**Sunday Staycation 23m Trad** Same flakes as Super Bowl Sunday. Instead of moving across slab continue up and right climbing through a corner. Finish at Sunday School belay. Rack to #2
3	5.10a	Take an Atheist to Church 20m Trad Starts left of Sunday School face climbing to gain slabs. Move across slab and through overhanging cracks to ledge. Belay via Sunday School. Rack small gear to #2

| 4 | 5.7 | **Sunday School 18m Trad** |

Start in low angled chimney to slab. Continue up left tending hand crack to corner to belay ledge.

Rack to #3

| 5 | 5.6 | **Slabbath 17m Trad** |

Climb slabs left of Easy Like Sunday. Finish moving left to Sunday School belay. Direct Var. 5.9PG13

Rack small gear to #2

| 6 | 5.5 | **Easy Like Sunday Morning 15m Trad** |

Climbs through obvious gully, finishing at Sunday School belay to the left.

Rack to #3

| 7 | 5.4 | **Easter Sunday 24m Trad** |

Starts in crack below slab and right of gully. Climb through the slab finishing at belay for Ritualistically Unclean.

Rack to #3

| 8 | 5.6 | **Ritualistically Unclean 23m Trad** |

Climb right side of varnished slab trending left. Finish straight up headwall to belay station.

Rack to #3

| 9 | 5.8 | **Thank God It's Monday 20m Trad** |

Began as for Ritualistically Unclean but continue straight up through left facing corner instead of climbing through the slab. Finish at belay station.

Rack to #3

3. SUNDAY WALL

| 10 | 5.10a | I Don't Roll On Shabbos 18m Top rope |

A TR route. Climbs steep head wall between Thank God It's Monday & Bloody Sunday.

| 11 | 5.8 | Bloody Sunday 21m Trad |

Left facing corner to bulging crack. Follow slab cracks to belay station.

Rack to #3

| 12 | 5.6 | Darkness on the Edge of Town 23m Trad |

A sizable corner at south end.

Rack to #3, optional #4

4. Basement/ Pass or Flail Ledge

Summary: 45+ min, Morning sun, Steep/ Overhung

Description: Stout test piece sport & trad lines.

Approach: Three options exist for access.

Option 1: Hike toward Sunday Wall. Once at ramp apex spot the sizable boulder and begin navigating down and around counter-clockwise from north side then cross small slab to gain lower tier. This is prior to reaching fixed cable traverse.

Option 2: From south end of Ashbury Park scramble down (~6') to ledge with anchors.

Option 3: N Alcove Schoolroom approach pitch.

1	5.13	CG's Project 15m Sport 6blt
2	5.12c	Propulsion 14m Sport 6blt
		Follows thin seam on upper varnished face left of Pass or Flail.
3	5.11d	Pass or Flail 14m Trad
		Classic route through shallow, flared jams leads to a bulge and insecure upper flared crack.
		Rack to #1
		FA: Greg Lowe, 1965
4	5.13a	I Got Stripes 12m Sport 5blt
		Seam through upper varnished face right of Pass or Flail
5	5.11b	Monkey Wrench 14m Sport 6blt
		Delicate moves on face then around arete.

4. Basement/ Pass or Flail Ledge

6	5.11d	Up & L 14m Sport 6blt

Overhanging start leads to slab above.

7	5.11b	Up & R 14m Sport 5blt

Thin powerful face & arête climbing.

8	5.4	Access Dihedral 12m Trad

Offers an alternative access for the 4x4 ledge, or egress from the Basement. See North Alcove approach.

Standard rack.

Summary: 45+ min, All Day Sun, Steep/Overhung

Description: An excellent selection of diverse climbing.

Approach: Continue past Sunday Wall to ramp apex. Traverse fixed cable to gain Ashbury Park ledges.

1 **5.12b** Detroit Muscle 12m Sport 4blt
Leftmost route, bouldery start through overhang finishing on moderate terrain.

2 **5.12b** Bound for Glory 18m Sport 7blt
Climbs arête left of face.

3 **5.12a** Badlands 18m Sport 6blt
5.10 climbing on face followed by bouldery one move wonder crux. Finishes left of arête joining Bound for Glory.

4 **5.13a** The Notion 18m Sport 6blt
-Direct finish variation, Badlands. Pull right through overhang, finishing on E Street upper face.

5 **5.10c** E Street 18m Trad
Ascend corner on north end of wall. Shares anchor with Bound for Glory.
Rack to #3.

6 **5.12a** Suicide Rap 14m Sport 5blt
Climbs large bulge.

7 **5.13b** Rule of Three 18m Sport 6blt
Climb Suicide Rap, finishing on right leaning seam to Thunder Road belay.

8   5.11d   **Thunder Road 18m Trad**
First obvious crack right of E Street. Variety of jams and bulge crux.
Small gear #0-2

9   5.12a   **Jungleland 17m Sport 6blt**
Near bolt 3 move left toward Thunder Road crack avoiding poor rock.

10   5.11d   **The Traditionalist 15m Trad**
Climb small roof and bulge above Flamingo Lane start using thin cracks.
Rack small gear to #1

11   5.7   **Flamingo Lane 14m Trad**
Right trending crack & flake features lead to belay ledge above Pocket Loverboy.
Rack to #3

12   5.8   **Colby's Crack Trad**
Direct start variation, Flamingo Lane. Crack right of Flamingo Lane start.
Rack to #3

13   5.11c   **Pocket Loverboy 12m Sport 4blt**
Great face climbing with unique finger pocket crux.

14   5.10b   **Stomach Your Fears 12m Sport 4blt**
Increasingly challenging climbing leads to crux at 4th bolt.

15   **Gangsta Ledge Access 8m**
Fixed rope on easy class 4/5 terrain to gain Upper Gangsta Ledge.

Looking north toward Gangsta Ledges, Catwalk, & Alcove. This is the access point for Catwalk from south end near Nightschool wall.

6. GANGSTA LEDGES

Summary: 45+ min, All Day Sun, Steep/Overhung

Description: Various climbs located along 2 tiers of ledges.

Approach:

Upper Ledge: Ascend fixed line in short corner south of Ashbury Park.

Lower Ledge: Several climbs are located in recess near fixed cable traverse south of Gangsta Ledge access.

Traverse 2nd fixed cable to more routes & for Catwalk access.

1   `5.11a/b`   Teardrops on the City 20m Sport 6blt
Steep juggy roof to exposed arete.

2   `5.13a`   Tiny Giants 14m Sport 6blt
Technical face climbing on crimps.

3   `5.10a PG`   A Country Mile 20m Trad
Corner right of Teardrops on the City. Moves left through roof. Shares anchor with Teardrops on the City
Rack small cams to #2.

4   `5.9`   Country Mile Var. 21m Trad
-Variation (5.9 PG), traverse right under roof to Giants of Science anchor.

5   `5.11b`   Giants of Science 14m Sport 6blt

6. GANGSTA LEDGES

6   **5.11a**   Father Roy 27m Trad

Climb through bulge using hand crack.

Rack to #2

Giants of Science or Lucky Town anchors.
Alternatively belay off ledge. Finish with Class III
traverse south along ledge or top out cliff with a
short pitch.

7   **5.11b**   Lucky Town 14m Sport 3blt

Stick Clip first bolt or bring a #1 and/or #2 to
protect initial moves.

8   **5.12a**   Rattlesnake Speedway 20m Sport 6blt

Small roof to large bulge with seam.

9   **5.10b**   Takeda Route 20m Trad 3blt

Last route encountered before southern cable
traverse. Lightning bolt crack, gear for lower
crack & upper seam.

Rack #0.5-2

10   **5.6**   Upper Alcove Access 6m Trad

Short route through left facing dihedral next to
Takeda Route gains Upper Alcove ledge. Build
natural or gear belay.

Rack to #3.

Catwalk Connection ledge is wider than it appears. Aim toward the boulder in the middle. It does require a few class III/IV moves throughout.

Summary: 60+ min, Afternoon Sun, Exposed, Late Shade, Water seepage

Description: Thin ledge within alcove connecting North & South portions of Schoolroom.

Approach:

Northern Routes 1-3: begin south of fixed cable traverse near Gangsta Ledge.

Southern Routes 4-8: begin off ledge accessed via short scramble near Night School wall.

1	5.11a	Clarence on the Sax 14m Trad
		Fingers to hands crack on left hand side.
		Rack to #3
2	5.11d	Maria's Bed 17m Sport 7blt
		Climbs multiple steep roofs.
3	5.12a	Little Early-Pearly 14m Sport 6blt
		Last route before Catwalk. Slabby with short bouldery crux near 4th bolt.
4	5.13a	Unknown 2 Sport
5	5.11c	Unknown 3 Sport
6	5.12c	Unknown 4 Sport
7	5.11b	BNF 8m Sport 4blt
8	5.12a	Unknown 5 8m Sport 5blt

8. Alcove

Summary: 90+min, Afternoon Sun, Exposed, Water seepage, Steep hike, Climb in

Description: A cliff sector located within middle, recessed region of Schoolroom and consists of the upper tier. Gangsta Ledges are north, Nightschool Wall south, and Catwalk below. Excellent summer climbing crag. Be aware water seepage after wet weather.

Approach:

Any Schoolroom approach will gain this section and require nearly equal time. If you venture this far you're a true Schoolroom climber!

1	5.10d	Unknown Left Sport 11blt

A king line for 5.10 climbing at the schoolroom. Crux at 2nd bolt, middle crux, and spicy finish. Great warm up for the area.

2	5.10c	Unknown Right Sport 11blt

Steady climbing through progressively difficult terrain. Crux is final moves. A must do 5.10.

3		Unknown 3 23m Sport 8blt
4	5.12b	Spicy Tuna Roll 14m Sport 7blt
5	5.13b	For Whom the Bell Tolls 15m Sport 8blt
6	5.12b	Postmodernism 20m Sport 7blt
7		Unknown 4 Sport

Stout arrete with at least 7 bolts.

8	5.11a	Clown'n Around 12m Sport 4blt

Climbs initial face through tough pinches. Finishes on No Talent A** Clown anchor.

9	5.11c	Face of Time 24m Sport 11blt

Upper head wall with crux near anchor. Originally started from Clown'n Around (9 bolts) but can linked from No Talent A** Clown (11 bolts).

10	5.10c	No Talent A** Clown 17m Sport 5blt

Decent moderate arrete climbing with tricky crux.

11		Unknown 5 Sport
12	5.11a	Bad to the Bone 27m Trad

Classic hand crack, option to finish on Universal Current.

Rack to #3

13	5.11a	Raktajino 27m Sport 8blt
14	5.7	Universal Current 27m Trad

Rack to #3

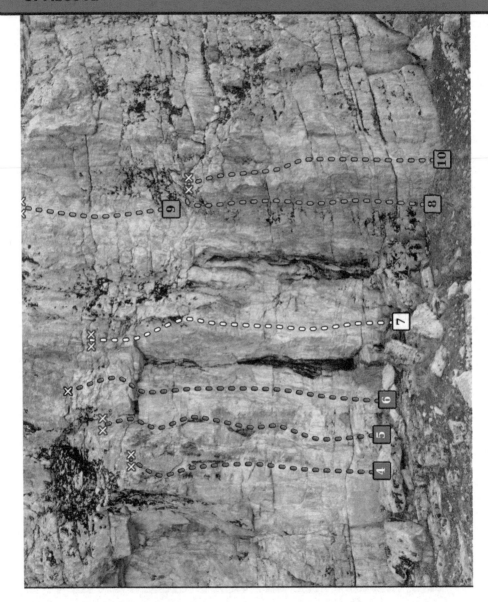

9. NightSchool

Summary: 90+min, Afternoon Sun, Exposed, Steep/Overhang, 70m rope

Description: First wall south of Alcove. This crag contains two levels. Upper routes begin left of Strange Relationship. Use extended slings for rope management. Best to belay followers from lower section.

Approach: Via Catwalk, Schoolroom south or Approach pitches.

1. **5.11a** Strange Relationship Sport 6blt
   Finishes straight to anchor on small pinnacle.
2. **5.12a** The Word Sport 8blt

   Dyno off the deck provides an exciting crux early.
3. **5.12c** Epitaph Sport 10blt
   Steady climbing leads to thoughtful crux on thin holds.
4. **5.12d** Overkill Sport 9blt
5. Black Sweat Sport 8blt
   Blank climbing on arete leads to 10+ climbing and more moderate climbing to finish. Possibly the most difficult sequence in Schoolroom.
6. **5.11c** Salary Man Sport 9blt

   Starts with small roof and finishes on bolted crack.
7. **5.12d** Splendid Isolation Sport 8blt
   Steep overhanging rock and bulges make up the first half of this challenging line.

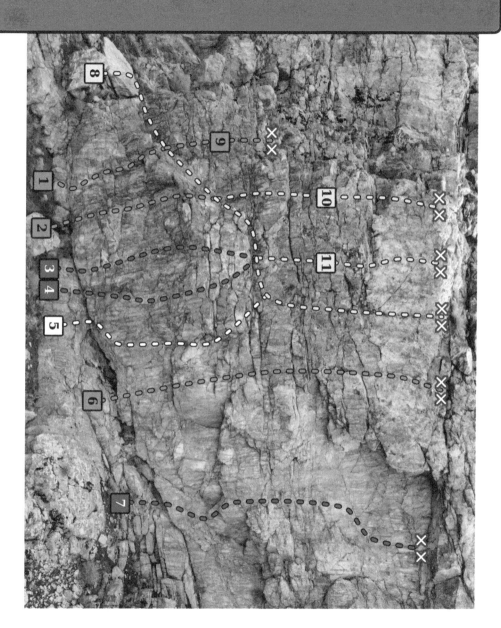

| 8 | 5.8 | After Hours Sport 8blt |

This line is used to access upper routes of Nightschool wall. Finishes on 4th bolt line up first crack encountered.

| 9 | 5.10b | Insomnia Sport 6blt |

Finishes on 1st bolt line leading to small pinnacle.

| 10 | 5.9 | Vacancy Sport 8blt |
| 11 | 5.10a | Night School Sport 10blt |

10. TANGERINE

Summary: 60+min, Afternoon Sun, Vertical

Description: Tangerine boasts a handful of excellent quality routes. Expect nice edges & in-cuts holds.

Approach:
Schoolroom south approaches.

1	5.7	Fist Full of Needles 23m Trad

Left facing dihedral north of the Tangerine. Climbs face with crack for protection. Gear belay on top, descend south using tree crack area repel stations.

Rack to #6, doubles 3-6.

2	5.11a	Verona 18m Sport 6blt

Excellent face climbing with reachy crux

3	5.10b	Excess Ain't Revellion 18m Trad

Rack to #1

4	5.11c	Collateral Damage 23m Sport 5blt

Rack #0.75- #2

5	5.11c	BLU-82 24m Sport 8blt

Crux finish that will leave you gassed.

11. 5.10 SLAB

Summary: 45+min, Late-morning sun, Vertical/Slab

Description: This wall offers a great introduction for Schoolroom 5.10 sport climbing.

Approach:
Schoolroom south approaches.

1	5.10b	Ladybug 15m Sport 5blt
2	5.10c	Mantis 15m Sport 4blt
3	5.10a	Body Count 18m Sport 6blt
4	5.10d	Attack on America 18m Sport 6blt

12. GREAT FLAKE

Summary: 45+min, Late-morning sun, Vertical, Runout, Exposed

Description: Quality sport lines providing a worthwhile introduction to Schoolroom climbing.

Approach: Schoolroom south approaches.

1	5.12c	Tigers on Vaseline 18m Sport 3blt
		Follow arete on northern end of Great Flake. Stout climbing off deck leads to moderate terrain. Stick clip recommended.
2	5.12a	Mercury Topaz 18m Sport 6blt
3	5.10c	Mr. Styles 18m Sport 5blt
		Begin in left facing corner flakes continuing up face.
4	5.11c	Lickety Split 18m Sport 7blt
5	5.10b	All Quite on the Western Front 15m Sport 5blt
		Opt. small/medium nuts
6	5.9	Rehab's For Quitters 15m Sport 5blt
7	5.10c	South Ridge Direct 18m Trad 1blt
		1 bolt for start crux.
		Rack to #3.
8	5.6	South Ridge 18m Trad
		Climb cracks up & around arete.
		Rack to #3

13. TREE CRACK

Summary: 45+min, Late-morning sun, Vertical, Cracks, Runout, Exposed

Description: Named after the historic Lowe route, this crag hosts a variety of fun challenging lines.

Approach:

Schoolroom south approaches.

1	5.10b R	Psycho Corner Trad
		Climb through ledges & flakes to splinter hand crack. Be cautious of loos blocks on topout.
2	5.12a	Goodbye Blue Monday 18m Sport 6blt
		Opt. nuts or small cams
3	5.12d	Breakfast of Champions 18m Sport 5blt
4	5.11a	Tree Crack 24m Trad
		Rack small to #2.
5	5.10d	Tastes Like Burning 23m Sport 6blt
		Opt. #1
6	5.12c	The Wasp 20m Sport 7blt
7	5.9	Macondo 25m Trad
		Climb to ledge at start of route. Trend left following flakes and ledges aiming for the upper corner.
		Rack to #3
8	5.12a	Rockprodigy 15m Sport 5blt
9	5.11d	Explosivo 23m Sport 10blt

13. TREE CRACK

10	5.12d	Castrated Stalker 18m Sport 6blt
		Var. pitch 2 finish (5.9): Continue from belay up left trending crack finishing on Shiny Demon.
		Rack to #2
11	5.9	Shiny Demon Trad
		Alternate finish to Solar Flare & Rocketsauce. Traverse right along crack intersecting Rocketsauce at 8th bolt. 1 or 2 pitches.
		Rack to #3
12	5.11c	Rocketsauce 29m Sport 10blt
13	5.10d	Creamgenes 21m Trad
		Direct finish for Solar Flare
14	5.10c/d	Solar Flare 25m Trad
		Rack to #2
		Var. (10dR): direct variation.
15	5.11c	Phat Abbot 15m Sport 6blt
16	5.10b R	Jammin for Jesus 15m Trad
		Small nuts/ micro cams to #2
17	5.9 PG	Ethics 23m Trad 3
		Mixed route starting with 3 bolts.
		Rack to #3

(Topo pg 67)

Summary: 45+min, Late-morning sun, Cracks, Bushwacking, Chossy

Description: These routes are seldom climbed but can be used as approach pitches. They are found along the lower cliff band and tops out on the main 4X4 ledge

Approach: Access by traversing north from Utahnic wall or navigate boulder field below Alcove and head south along lower cliff band. Some bushwacking required.

1   5.7   Approach Crack 20m Trad

Approach as for Utahnics and continue north along base. Locate Tree Crack and find moderate crack. Belay off single bolt.
Rack to #3.

2   5.10b   Corner Overhang Var. 1 Trad

Climbs below prominent overhang.
Climb west face right of overhang (PG13).
Rack to #3

3   5.11d   Var. 2 Trad

Climb slab to corner in the back of overhang.
Move right on horizontal crack beneath roof.
Rack to #3

4   5.11d   Var. 3 Trad

Climb up and left to left most corner of the roof. Travers under roof walking cams. Exiting roof is the crux for variations 2 & 3.

5   5.9 PG   Strange Behavior Trad

Climb corner toward large detached block. Finish on diagonal finger to hand crack. Be mindful of sharp corners.

Rack to #4, double #1-#3

6   Fixed Line

Below the Great Flake is a fixed line to access lower class broken terrain and gain 4X4 ledge.

15. UTAHNICS

Summary: 45+min, Afternoon sun, Cracks,

Description: A popular crag due to its less committing access. Located atop the talus field, Utahnics offer a variety of moderate climbing.

Approach: Schoolroom south approach.

1	5.12a	Hype Dependant 12m Sport 4blt
2	5.9	Diamondback 12m Trad
		Nuts and cams to #1
3	5.10a	Utahnics 12m Sport 5blt
4	5.8	Holy Moroni 12m Sport 5blt
5	5.8	Oh My Nephi 12m Sport 5blt
		Var. Nephi Direct (5.8): Climbs through bulge, generally left as a top rope.
6	5.7	Telestrial 12m Trad
		Rack to #3
7	5.8	Terrestrial 12m Trad
		Rack to #3
8	5.6	The Good Ward 12m Trad
		Rack to #2.
9	5.7	Celestial 12m Trad
		Rack to #3

16. Taylor's Corner

Summary: 45+min, Afternoon sun, Cracks, Chossy, Runout

Description: Somewhat vague, test piece trad lines located above Utahnics.

Approach: Schoolroom south approach.

1	5.11b R	**Drop Zone 37m Trad**
		An ambiguous and notorious Greg Lowe route ascending a right arching corner above Utahnic wall ranging from ~10R-11+X depending on line.
		Standard rack, singles to #1, doubles #1-#3
		Descent: Walk north to Tree Crack sector and repel from summit tree or anchors at lip.
2	Unknown	**27th Street Overhang Trad**
		A little know route climbing an obvious feature......
3	5.8	**Taylor's Corner 30m Trad**
		Start on face south of large right facing corner. Pass pitons continuing up and left finishing through upper dihedral.
		Rack to #3
4	5.10c	**Box Elder Salsa 26m Trad**
		Start in large corner south of 27th Overhang.
5	5.11c R	**Laurel 27m Trad**
		5.8 C2. Thin seem through face. Moderate climbing to topout.
		Standard rack, multiple of small cams & nuts.

Summary: 45+min, Morning sun, Chossy, Runout, Exposed, Windy, Toprope accessible

Description: A unique addition to Schoolroom's offerings featuring 3 levels for climbing. Here you will find an assortment of trad, sport, mixed & multipitch lines. Some routes require 70m ropes.

Approach: Approach as for Utahnics wall. Head right along base toward (41.217593, -111.922605)

1	5.8	Drop the hammer Trad
2	5.10b	Cosmic chain if Events Sport
3	5.8	Anna Trad
		Begins in corner & climbs to rim.
		rack to #3
4	5.9	Filling up the Basement Sport
5	5.10c	Upstairs at the Front Sport
6	5.9	Doing it for the O Trad 4blt
		Follow alternating bolts & horizontal breaks.
		Rack to #2
7	5.10a	Trophy Husband Club Trad 1blt
		Clip a lone bolt continuing up face using breaks & bods for protection.
		Rack to #2
8	5.9	The Old Way Trad
		Climb corner to ledge then move left through breaks & pods.
		Rack to #3

Schoolroom South Buttress

17. Southern Buttress

9	5.10c	Rope Thief 17m Trad 4
		Climb corner then follow first set of bolts on upper headwall.
		Rack to #2
10	5.10d	Forgotten Highness Sport
11	5.10a	Under the nose of the Reaper Sport
		Great warmup for the area be careful of block toward top of route.

17. SOUTHERN BUTTRESS, COUPLER AREA

2	5.8	Snail Trail Trad
		Rack to #3, 70m rope.
3	5.8	Avoiding the Sting Trad
		Rack to #3, 70m rope.
4	5.10a	Thank my Wife Sport
5	5.8	Young Handsome & Strapping Trad
		Breaks & pods lead to corner.
		Rack to #2
6	5.7	Probably a Lowe Trad
		Rack to #2
7	5.6	Destined for Obscurity Trad
		Rack to #3

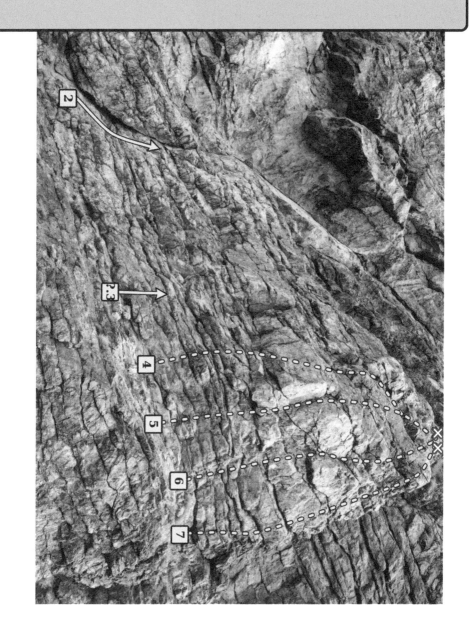

17. SOUTHERN BUTTRESS, So Ex

1	5.11c	Unknown 1 Sport
2	5.11b	Unknown 2 Sport
3	5.10c	Unknown 3 Sport
4	5.11.a	Total Consumption of the Mind Sport

1	5.11c	Unknow 1 Sport
		70m rope.
2	5.8	Snail Trail Trad
		Multipitch climbing through large corner (pg84).
		Rack to #3, 70m rope.
3	5.8	Avoiding the Sting Trad
		Alt. Finish for Snail Trail (pg84).
		Rack to #3, 70m rope.
3	5.8	Anna Trad
		Begins in corner & climbs to rim (pg83).
		rack to #3
8	5.10d	Snake Eyes Sport
		Further right from main wall. Follows a steep arete & headwall, 70m rope.
9	5.7	Merciful Snake Trad (not pictured)
		Snake Eyes var. finish. Move left at the start of pitch 2 through small corner. Move back right to gain pitch 2 anchor.
		Rack to #2, 70m rope.

SO EX

Coupler Area

Center Stage

89

19 Class III/IV 4x4 Ledge Traverse Via ferrata

Traversing Schoolroom offers a leisurely Via Ferrata style outing including fixed cable traverses, repels, a catwalk & light scrambling. Common options include a full traverse or partial traverse with a loop at the alcove. See pg 39 & 43.

20 5.10d Castle Rock 9m Trad 2blt

Bouldery steep face climbing. Excellent for the grade and great top rope route. Boulders along base make this PG-13/R for leading. Several variations 10+ to 11 range. (41.2173292, -111.9257018)

Rack #0.4-#2

20

To-Do list

	4x4 ledge Traverse	90
	Schoolroom Ridge Trad	12
5.5	Easy Like Sunday Morning 15m Trad	26
5.6	South Ridge 18m Trad	64
	Darkness on the Edge of Town 23m Trad	30
	Upper Alcove Access 6m Trad	42
5.7	Universal Current 27m Trad	52
	Phantasmagorical var. 18m Sport	18
	Flamingo Lane 14m Trad	38
	Telestrial 12m Trad	76
	Sunday School 18m Trad	26
5.8	After Hours Sport	58
	Terrestrial 12m Trad	76
	Anna Trad	80
	Oh My Nephi 12m Sport	76
	Bloody Sunday 21m Trad	30
5.9	Lunch Box RIP 15m Sport	16
	Vacancy Sport	58
	Rehab's For Quitters 15m Sport	64
	Diamondback 12m Trad	76
	Ethics 23m Trad	70

INDEX OF ROUTES BY GRADE

Grade	Route		Page
5.7	Probably a Lowe Trad		84
	Merciful Snake Trad		88
5.8	Thank God It's Monday 20m Trad		26
	Bloody Sunday 21m Trad		30
	Colby's Crack Trad		38
	After Hours Sport		58
	Holy Moroni 12m Sport		76
	Oh My Nephi 12m Sport		76
	Terrestrial 12m Trad		76
	Taylor's Corner 30m Trad		78
	Drop the hammer Trad		80
	Anna Trad		80
	Snail Trail Trad		84,88
	Avoiding the Sting Trad		84,88
	Young Handsome & Strapping Trad		84
5.9	Lunch Box RIP 15m Sport		16
	Homecoming Princess 18m Sport		18
	Blue Steel 18m Sport		18
	Phantasmagorical Direct 18m Sport		18
	Country Mile Var. 21m Trad		40
	Vacancy Sport		58
	Rehab's For Quitters 15m Sport		64
	Macondo 25m Trad		68
	Shiny Demon Trad		70
	Diamondback 12m Trad		76
	Filling up the Basement Sport		80
	Doing it for the O Trad		80

Grade	Route		Page
5.10b	Cosmic chain if Events Sport		80,88
5.10b R	Psycho Corner Trad		68
	Jammin for Jesus 15m Trad		70
5.10c	E Street 18m Trad		36
	Unknown Right Sport		50
	No Talent A** Clown 17m Sport		52
	Mantis 15m Sport		62
	Mr. Styles 18m Sport		64
	South Ridge Direct 18m Trad		64
	Box Elder Salsa 26m Trad		78
	Upstairs at the Front Sport		80
	Rope Thief 17m Trad		82
	Unknown 3 Sport		86
5.10d	Castle Rock 9m Trad		90
	Unknown Left Sport		50
	Attack on America 18m Sport		62
	Tastes Like Burning 23m Sport		68
	Creamgenes 21m Trad		70
	Forgotten Highness Sport		82
	Snake Eyes Sport		88
5.10+	Solar Flare 25m Trad		70
5.10d/11a			16
	Love Peace Weed 15m Sport		
5.11a	Father Roy 27m Trad		42
	Clarence on the Sax 14m Trad		44
	Clown'n Around 12m Sport		50
	Bad to the Bone 27m Trad		52
	Raktajino 27m Sport		52

Grade	Route	Number
5.11d	Pass or Flail 14m Trad	32
	Up & L 14m Sport	34
	Thunder Road 18m Trad	36
	The Traditionalist 15m Trad	38
	Maria's Bed 17m Sport	44
	Explosivo 23m Sport	68
	Var. 2 Trad	72
	Var. 3 Trad	72
5.12a	MIA 18m Sport	16
	Badlands 18m Sport	36
	Suicide Rap 14m Sport	36
	Jungleland 17m Sport	38
	Rattlesnake	42
	Speedway 20m Sport	
	Little Early-Pearly 14m Sport	44
	Unknown 5 8m Sport	44
	The Word Sport	56
	Mercury Topaz 18m Sport	64
	Goodbye Blue Monday 18m Sport	68
	Rockprodigy 15m Sport	68
	Hype Dependant 12m Sport	76
5.12b	Detroit Muscle 12m Sport	36
	Bound for Glory 18m Sport	36
	Spicy Tuna Roll 14m Sport	50
	Postmodernism 20m Sport	50
5.12c	Propulsion 14m Sport	32
	Unknown 4 Sport	44
	Epitaph Sport	56

INDEX OF ROUTES BY GRADE

NOTES:

Gerald Consulting Services

-Offering a full suite of solar, renewable energy, and energy storage systems, designs & services

-Will match or beat competitor pricing for standard grid-tied residential systems

- Portion of proceeds go toward charitable projects

- Pricing start $2.80-$3/watt

- Support local enterprises

Ph: (801)336-7469

FB: GeraldConsultingServices

TheCrag's mission is to build an enduring resource of the world's climbing information, to facilitate sustainable climbing and to support a thriving community.

Our vision is being the number one climbing platform worldwide and in all key climbing countries individually as well as being the market leader with respect to user satisfaction, data quality, completeness, technological leadership and sustainable behaviour.

The climbing community and theCrag depend on YOU to achieve these goals.

www.thecrag.com

Made in the USA
Columbia, SC
29 September 2022